50 Wild Harvest Recipes for Home

By: Kelly Johnson

Table of Contents

- Foraged Mushroom Risotto
- Dandelion Greens Salad
- Wild Berry Jam
- Stinging Nettle Soup
- Elderflower Cordial
- Wild Herb Pesto
- Acorn Flour Pancakes
- Chickweed Salad
- Wild Garlic Butter
- Fiddlehead Fern Sauté
- Pine Needle Tea
- Wild Cherry Pie
- Cattail Root Fritters
- Berry-Stuffed Crepes
- Lamb's Quarters Stir-Fry
- Wild Mint Mojito
- Sassafras Root Beer
- Burdock Root Chips
- Wild Plum Chutney
- Milkweed Pod Tacos
- Hawthorn Berry Jelly
- Ground Cherry Salsa
- Wild Rose Petal Jam
- Wild Carrot Fritters
- Sea Beet Salad
- Spruce Tip Syrup
- Chickweed Pesto
- Sunchoke Mash
- Wildflower Salad
- Burdock Root Soup
- Goldenrod Tea
- Wild Blueberry Crisp
- Wild Radish Pickles
- Sweet Fern Cookies
- Hazelnut Crust Tart

- Wild Apple Cider
- Cattail Salad
- Spicy Wild Mustard Greens
- Wild Violet Salad
- Chanterelle Mushroom Tart
- Wild Raspberry Smoothie
- Oak Leaf Lettuce Wraps
- Wild Fennel Risotto
- Dandelion Wine
- Pickled Wild Onions
- Wildflower Honey Cake
- Pine Cone Jelly
- Wild Celery Root Gratin
- Sweet Potato and Foraged Greens Casserole
- Wild Sage Cornbread

Foraged Mushroom Risotto

Ingredients

- **1 cup** Arborio rice
- **4 cups** vegetable broth
- **1 cup** foraged mushrooms, chopped
- **½ cup** onion, diced
- **2 cloves** garlic, minced
- **¼ cup** white wine (optional)
- **¼ cup** grated Parmesan cheese
- **2 tbsp** olive oil
- **Salt and pepper** to taste
- **Fresh herbs** (like parsley) for garnish

Instructions

1. **Sauté Aromatics**: In a pot, heat olive oil and sauté onion and garlic until soft. Add mushrooms and cook until tender.
2. **Toast Rice**: Stir in Arborio rice and cook for 1-2 minutes. If using, add white wine and let it absorb.
3. **Add Broth**: Gradually add warm vegetable broth, stirring frequently, until rice is creamy and al dente (about 18-20 minutes). Stir in Parmesan and season to taste. Garnish with fresh herbs.

Dandelion Greens Salad

Ingredients

- **2 cups** dandelion greens, washed and torn
- **½ cup** cherry tomatoes, halved
- **¼ cup** red onion, thinly sliced
- **¼ cup** feta cheese, crumbled
- **¼ cup** olive oil
- **2 tbsp** balsamic vinegar
- **Salt and pepper** to taste

Instructions

1. **Prepare Dressing**: In a small bowl, whisk together olive oil, balsamic vinegar, salt, and pepper.
2. **Combine Salad Ingredients**: In a large bowl, toss dandelion greens, cherry tomatoes, red onion, and feta.
3. **Dress Salad**: Drizzle dressing over salad and toss gently before serving.

Wild Berry Jam

Ingredients

- **2 cups** wild berries (like blackberries or raspberries)
- **1 cup** sugar
- **1 tbsp** lemon juice
- **1 tbsp** pectin (optional for thicker jam)

Instructions

1. **Cook Berries**: In a saucepan, combine berries, sugar, and lemon juice. Cook over medium heat until berries break down (about 10-15 minutes).
2. **Thicken (Optional)**: Stir in pectin if desired and cook for another 5 minutes until thickened.
3. **Cool and Store**: Pour into sterilized jars and let cool before sealing. Store in the fridge.

Stinging Nettle Soup

Ingredients

- **2 cups** stinging nettles, washed and chopped
- **1 cup** potato, diced
- **1 cup** onion, chopped
- **4 cups** vegetable broth
- **2 tbsp** olive oil
- **Salt and pepper** to taste
- **Cream or yogurt** for serving (optional)

Instructions

1. **Sauté Vegetables**: In a pot, heat olive oil and sauté onion until translucent. Add potatoes and cook for a few more minutes.
2. **Add Broth and Nettles**: Pour in vegetable broth and bring to a boil. Add nettles and simmer for 15-20 minutes until everything is tender.
3. **Blend and Serve**: Blend until smooth, season to taste, and serve with a swirl of cream or yogurt.

Elderflower Cordial

Ingredients

- **15-20 elderflower heads**
- **1 liter** water
- **1 kg** sugar
- **2 lemons,** sliced
- **1 tsp** citric acid

Instructions

1. **Prepare Elderflowers**: Gently rinse elderflower heads and place in a large bowl.
2. **Make Syrup**: In a pot, heat water and dissolve sugar. Pour over elderflowers. Add lemon slices and citric acid.
3. **Infuse**: Cover and let steep for 24 hours. Strain and bottle. Store in the fridge.

Wild Herb Pesto

Ingredients

- **2 cups** mixed wild herbs (like wild garlic, nettles, or parsley)
- **½ cup** nuts (like walnuts or pine nuts)
- **¼ cup** Parmesan cheese, grated
- **½ cup** olive oil
- **1 clove** garlic
- **Salt and pepper** to taste

Instructions

1. **Blend Ingredients**: In a food processor, combine herbs, nuts, Parmesan, garlic, and a pinch of salt. Pulse until chopped.
2. **Add Oil**: With the processor running, slowly drizzle in olive oil until smooth. Season to taste.

Acorn Flour Pancakes

Ingredients

- **1 cup** acorn flour
- **1 tsp** baking powder
- **¼ tsp** salt
- **1 cup** milk (or plant-based milk)
- **1 large egg**
- **2 tbsp** maple syrup or honey

Instructions

1. **Mix Dry Ingredients**: In a bowl, whisk together acorn flour, baking powder, and salt.
2. **Combine Wet Ingredients**: In another bowl, mix milk, egg, and maple syrup.
3. **Combine & Cook**: Gradually add wet to dry. Cook pancakes on a heated skillet until bubbles form, then flip and cook until golden brown.

Chickweed Salad

Ingredients

- **2 cups** chickweed, washed and chopped
- **½ cup** cucumber, diced
- **½ cup** cherry tomatoes, halved
- **¼ cup** feta cheese, crumbled
- **2 tbsp** olive oil
- **1 tbsp** lemon juice
- **Salt and pepper** to taste

Instructions

1. **Prepare Dressing**: In a small bowl, whisk together olive oil, lemon juice, salt, and pepper.
2. **Combine Salad Ingredients**: In a large bowl, mix chickweed, cucumber, cherry tomatoes, and feta.
3. **Dress Salad**: Drizzle dressing over salad and toss gently before serving.

Enjoy your foraged delights!

Wild Garlic Butter

Ingredients

- **1 cup** unsalted butter, softened
- **½ cup** wild garlic leaves, chopped
- **Salt** to taste

Instructions

1. **Mix Ingredients**: In a bowl, combine softened butter, wild garlic, and salt. Mix until well combined.
2. **Chill**: Transfer to parchment paper, shape into a log, and chill in the fridge until firm. Use as a spread or in cooking.

Fiddlehead Fern Sauté

Ingredients

- **2 cups** fiddlehead ferns, cleaned
- **2 tbsp** olive oil
- **2 cloves** garlic, minced
- **Salt and pepper** to taste
- **Lemon juice** (optional)

Instructions

1. **Sauté Fiddles**: In a pan, heat olive oil and add fiddlehead ferns. Sauté for 5-7 minutes until tender.
2. **Add Garlic**: Stir in garlic and cook for another minute. Season with salt, pepper, and a squeeze of lemon juice before serving.

Pine Needle Tea

Ingredients

- **1 cup** fresh pine needles, chopped
- **4 cups** water
- **Honey** (optional)

Instructions

1. **Boil Water**: In a pot, bring water to a boil.
2. **Steep**: Add chopped pine needles and reduce heat. Simmer for 10-15 minutes. Strain and sweeten with honey if desired.

Wild Cherry Pie

Ingredients

- **2 cups** wild cherries, pitted
- **¾ cup** sugar
- **1 tbsp** cornstarch
- **1 tsp** vanilla extract
- **1 pre-made pie crust**

Instructions

1. **Prepare Filling**: In a bowl, mix cherries, sugar, cornstarch, and vanilla.
2. **Assemble Pie**: Pour filling into pie crust and cover with a second crust. Cut slits for steam.
3. **Bake**: Bake at 375°F (190°C) for 30-35 minutes until golden. Cool before serving.

Cattail Root Fritters

Ingredients

- **1 cup** cattail roots, grated
- **½ cup** all-purpose flour
- **1 egg**
- **Salt and pepper** to taste
- **Oil for frying**

Instructions

1. **Mix Batter**: In a bowl, combine grated cattail roots, flour, egg, salt, and pepper.
2. **Fry Fritters**: Heat oil in a pan and drop spoonfuls of batter. Fry until golden brown on both sides. Drain on paper towels.

Berry-Stuffed Crepes

Ingredients

- **1 cup** all-purpose flour
- **2 eggs**
- **1 ½ cups** milk
- **2 tbsp** melted butter
- **1 cup** mixed berries (fresh or frozen)
- **Powdered sugar** for serving

Instructions

1. **Make Crepe Batter**: Whisk flour, eggs, milk, and melted butter until smooth. Let rest for 30 minutes.
2. **Cook Crepes**: Heat a non-stick pan and pour in batter, swirling to coat. Cook until golden, then flip.
3. **Stuff and Serve**: Fill crepes with berries, fold, and sprinkle with powdered sugar.

Lamb's Quarters Stir-Fry

Ingredients

- **2 cups** lamb's quarters, washed and chopped
- **1 cup** mixed vegetables (like bell peppers and carrots)
- **2 tbsp** soy sauce
- **1 tbsp** sesame oil
- **1 clove** garlic, minced

Instructions

1. **Heat Oil**: In a pan, heat sesame oil over medium heat.
2. **Stir-Fry Vegetables**: Add mixed vegetables and garlic, cooking until tender. Add lamb's quarters and soy sauce, cooking for another 2-3 minutes until wilted.

Wild Mint Mojito

Ingredients

- **10 fresh mint leaves**
- **1 tbsp** sugar
- **1 lime,** juiced
- **1 cup** soda water
- **Ice**

Instructions

1. **Muddle Mint**: In a glass, muddle mint leaves and sugar together.
2. **Add Lime**: Squeeze in lime juice and stir.
3. **Mix**: Fill the glass with ice and top with soda water. Stir gently and enjoy!

Enjoy these wild and delicious creations!

Sassafras Root Beer

Ingredients

- **2 cups** sassafras root, chopped
- **4 cups** water
- **1 cup** sugar
- **1 tbsp** vanilla extract
- **1 tsp** yeast (optional for fermentation)

Instructions

1. **Boil Sassafras**: In a pot, combine sassafras root and water. Boil for 20-30 minutes.
2. **Strain and Sweeten**: Strain the liquid and stir in sugar and vanilla extract. If fermenting, add yeast and let sit for 24 hours.
3. **Chill**: Refrigerate and serve chilled.

Burdock Root Chips

Ingredients

- **1 large burdock root,** peeled and thinly sliced
- **2 tbsp** olive oil
- **Salt** to taste

Instructions

1. **Preheat Oven**: Preheat to 375°F (190°C).
2. **Toss and Bake**: Toss burdock slices with olive oil and salt. Spread on a baking sheet in a single layer.
3. **Bake**: Bake for 25-30 minutes until crispy, turning halfway. Cool before serving.

Wild Plum Chutney

Ingredients

- **2 cups** wild plums, pitted and chopped
- **½ cup** onion, diced
- **1 cup** sugar
- **½ cup** vinegar
- **1 tsp** ginger, grated
- **1 tsp** cinnamon

Instructions

1. **Combine Ingredients**: In a pot, combine plums, onion, sugar, vinegar, ginger, and cinnamon.
2. **Cook Down**: Simmer over medium heat for 30-40 minutes until thickened. Stir occasionally.
3. **Cool and Store**: Let cool and store in jars. Use as a condiment.

Milkweed Pod Tacos

Ingredients

- **1 cup** milkweed pods, cooked and chopped
- **½ cup** onion, diced
- **1 tsp** cumin
- **Salt and pepper** to taste
- **Taco shells** (soft or hard)

Instructions

1. **Sauté Filling**: In a pan, sauté onion until translucent. Add chopped milkweed pods, cumin, salt, and pepper. Cook for 5-7 minutes.
2. **Assemble Tacos**: Fill taco shells with the milkweed mixture and top with your choice of toppings.

Hawthorn Berry Jelly

Ingredients

- **2 cups** hawthorn berries
- **1 cup** water
- **¾ cup** sugar
- **1 tbsp** lemon juice
- **1 tbsp** pectin (optional)

Instructions

1. **Cook Berries**: In a pot, combine hawthorn berries and water. Simmer for 30 minutes until soft.
2. **Strain**: Strain the mixture through a fine sieve, pressing to extract juice.
3. **Make Jelly**: Return juice to the pot, stir in sugar, lemon juice, and pectin if using. Boil for 5-10 minutes. Pour into jars and seal.

Ground Cherry Salsa

Ingredients

- **1 cup** ground cherries, husked and diced
- **½ cup** onion, diced
- **1 jalapeño,** minced (optional)
- **Juice of 1 lime**
- **Salt** to taste
- **Cilantro** (optional)

Instructions

1. **Combine Ingredients**: In a bowl, mix ground cherries, onion, jalapeño, lime juice, salt, and cilantro.
2. **Chill and Serve**: Let sit for 15 minutes to meld flavors. Serve with tortilla chips or as a topping.

Wild Rose Petal Jam

Ingredients

- **2 cups** wild rose petals, cleaned
- **2 cups** sugar
- **1 cup** water
- **Juice of 1 lemon**
- **1 tbsp** pectin (optional)

Instructions

1. **Make Syrup**: In a pot, combine water and sugar. Bring to a boil until dissolved.
2. **Add Petals**: Stir in rose petals and lemon juice. Simmer for 10-15 minutes.
3. **Set and Store**: Add pectin if using and boil for a few more minutes. Pour into jars and seal.

Wild Carrot Fritters

Ingredients

- **1 cup** wild carrot (Queen Anne's Lace) roots, grated
- **½ cup** all-purpose flour
- **1 egg**
- **Salt and pepper** to taste
- **Oil for frying**

Instructions

1. **Mix Batter**: In a bowl, combine grated wild carrot, flour, egg, salt, and pepper.
2. **Fry Fritters**: Heat oil in a pan and drop spoonfuls of batter. Fry until golden brown on both sides. Drain on paper towels.

Enjoy your wild culinary creations!

Sea Beet Salad

Ingredients

- **2 cups** sea beets, cleaned and chopped
- **1 cup** cherry tomatoes, halved
- **½ cup** feta cheese, crumbled
- **¼ cup** olive oil
- **2 tbsp** lemon juice
- **Salt and pepper** to taste

Instructions

1. **Blanch Sea Beets**: Bring a pot of salted water to a boil. Add sea beets and blanch for 2-3 minutes. Drain and cool.
2. **Combine Ingredients**: In a large bowl, mix sea beets, cherry tomatoes, and feta.
3. **Dress Salad**: Whisk together olive oil, lemon juice, salt, and pepper. Drizzle over the salad and toss gently.

Spruce Tip Syrup

Ingredients

- **1 cup** spruce tips, cleaned
- **1 cup** water
- **1 cup** sugar

Instructions

1. **Boil Ingredients**: In a pot, combine spruce tips, water, and sugar. Bring to a boil.
2. **Simmer**: Reduce heat and simmer for 15-20 minutes. Strain into a jar and let cool.
3. **Store**: Keep in the refrigerator and use as a sweetener or syrup.

Chickweed Pesto

Ingredients

- **2 cups** chickweed, washed and chopped
- **½ cup** nuts (like walnuts or pine nuts)
- **¼ cup** Parmesan cheese, grated
- **½ cup** olive oil
- **1 clove** garlic
- **Salt and pepper** to taste

Instructions

1. **Blend Ingredients**: In a food processor, combine chickweed, nuts, Parmesan, garlic, and a pinch of salt. Pulse until chopped.
2. **Add Oil**: With the processor running, slowly drizzle in olive oil until smooth. Adjust seasoning to taste.

Sunchoke Mash

Ingredients

- **2 cups** sunchokes, peeled and chopped
- **2 tbsp** butter
- **¼ cup** milk (or plant-based milk)
- **Salt and pepper** to taste

Instructions

1. **Boil Sunchokes**: In a pot, cover sunchokes with water and boil until tender (about 15-20 minutes). Drain.
2. **Mash**: In a bowl, mash sunchokes with butter, milk, salt, and pepper until smooth.

Wildflower Salad

Ingredients

- **2 cups** mixed wildflowers (edible varieties, like nasturtiums and violets), cleaned
- **1 cup** mixed greens
- **¼ cup** goat cheese, crumbled
- **¼ cup** olive oil
- **2 tbsp** balsamic vinegar
- **Salt and pepper** to taste

Instructions

1. **Combine Greens**: In a large bowl, combine wildflowers and mixed greens.
2. **Dress Salad**: Whisk together olive oil, balsamic vinegar, salt, and pepper. Drizzle over the salad and toss gently. Top with goat cheese.

Burdock Root Soup

Ingredients

- **1 cup** burdock root, peeled and diced
- **½ cup** onion, chopped
- **2 cloves** garlic, minced
- **4 cups** vegetable broth
- **2 tbsp** olive oil
- **Salt and pepper** to taste

Instructions

1. **Sauté Aromatics**: In a pot, heat olive oil and sauté onion and garlic until translucent. Add burdock root and cook for 5 minutes.
2. **Add Broth**: Pour in vegetable broth and bring to a boil. Reduce heat and simmer for 20 minutes until burdock is tender. Blend until smooth, then season to taste.

Goldenrod Tea

Ingredients

- **1 cup** fresh goldenrod flowers (or 2 tbsp dried)
- **2 cups** boiling water
- **Honey** (optional)

Instructions

1. **Steep Flowers**: Place goldenrod flowers in a teapot and pour boiling water over them. Steep for 10-15 minutes.
2. **Strain and Serve**: Strain the tea into cups and sweeten with honey if desired.

Wild Blueberry Crisp

Ingredients

- **2 cups** wild blueberries
- **½ cup** oats
- **½ cup** all-purpose flour
- **¼ cup** brown sugar
- **¼ cup** butter, melted
- **1 tsp** cinnamon

Instructions

1. **Preheat Oven**: Preheat to 350°F (175°C).
2. **Prepare Filling**: In a baking dish, combine wild blueberries and a sprinkle of sugar (if desired).
3. **Make Topping**: In a bowl, mix oats, flour, brown sugar, melted butter, and cinnamon until crumbly. Sprinkle over blueberries.
4. **Bake**: Bake for 25-30 minutes until bubbly and golden. Serve warm.

Enjoy your foraged and flavorful dishes!

Wild Radish Pickles

Ingredients

- **2 cups** wild radishes, sliced
- **1 cup** vinegar (white or apple cider)
- **1 cup** water
- **½ cup** sugar
- **1 tbsp** salt
- **1 tsp** mustard seeds (optional)

Instructions

1. **Prepare Brine**: In a pot, combine vinegar, water, sugar, and salt. Bring to a boil until sugar dissolves.
2. **Pack Radishes**: Place sliced radishes in a clean jar, adding mustard seeds if desired.
3. **Pour Brine**: Pour hot brine over radishes, ensuring they are fully submerged. Seal and let cool before refrigerating for at least 24 hours.

Sweet Fern Cookies

Ingredients

- **1 cup** butter, softened
- **1 cup** sugar
- **2 cups** all-purpose flour
- **¼ cup** sweet fern leaves, finely chopped
- **1 egg**
- **1 tsp** vanilla extract
- **½ tsp** baking soda

Instructions

1. **Preheat Oven**: Preheat to 350°F (175°C).
2. **Mix Ingredients**: In a bowl, cream butter and sugar. Add egg and vanilla, then mix in flour, sweet fern, and baking soda.
3. **Shape Cookies**: Drop spoonfuls onto a baking sheet and flatten slightly.
4. **Bake**: Bake for 10-12 minutes until edges are golden. Cool on a wire rack.

Hazelnut Crust Tart

Ingredients

- **1 cup** hazelnuts, ground
- **½ cup** flour
- **¼ cup** sugar
- **½ cup** butter, melted
- **1 egg**

Instructions

1. **Preheat Oven**: Preheat to 350°F (175°C).
2. **Combine Crust Ingredients**: In a bowl, mix ground hazelnuts, flour, sugar, melted butter, and egg until a dough forms.
3. **Form Crust**: Press the mixture into a tart pan. Prick the bottom with a fork.
4. **Bake**: Bake for 15-20 minutes until lightly golden. Let cool before filling.

Wild Apple Cider

Ingredients

- **10-12 wild apples,** chopped (with skins)
- **4 cups** water
- **½ cup** sugar (optional)
- **Cinnamon sticks** (optional)

Instructions

1. **Combine Ingredients**: In a pot, combine chopped apples and water. Bring to a boil.
2. **Simmer**: Reduce heat and simmer for 30-40 minutes, mashing apples to release juice.
3. **Strain**: Strain the mixture through a fine sieve. Sweeten with sugar and add cinnamon sticks if desired. Serve warm or chilled.

Cattail Salad

Ingredients

- **1 cup** cattail shoots, cleaned and chopped
- **1 cup** mixed greens
- **½ cup** cherry tomatoes, halved
- **¼ cup** vinaigrette dressing

Instructions

1. **Prepare Salad**: In a bowl, combine chopped cattail shoots, mixed greens, and cherry tomatoes.
2. **Dress Salad**: Drizzle with vinaigrette and toss gently to combine.

Spicy Wild Mustard Greens

Ingredients

- **2 cups** wild mustard greens, washed and chopped
- **2 cloves** garlic, minced
- **2 tbsp** olive oil
- **1 tsp** red pepper flakes (adjust to taste)
- **Salt** to taste

Instructions

1. **Sauté Garlic**: In a pan, heat olive oil over medium heat. Add garlic and red pepper flakes, cooking until fragrant.
2. **Add Greens**: Stir in mustard greens and cook until wilted, about 5 minutes. Season with salt and serve.

Wild Violet Salad

Ingredients

- **2 cups** wild violet leaves and flowers, cleaned
- **1 cup** mixed greens
- **½ cup** goat cheese, crumbled
- **¼ cup** balsamic vinaigrette

Instructions

1. **Combine Greens**: In a large bowl, mix wild violets and mixed greens.
2. **Dress Salad**: Drizzle with balsamic vinaigrette and top with goat cheese. Toss gently before serving.

Chanterelle Mushroom Tart

Ingredients

- **2 cups** chanterelle mushrooms, cleaned and sliced
- **1 cup** heavy cream
- **3 eggs**
- **½ cup** cheese (like Gruyère), grated
- **1 prepared pie crust**
- **Salt and pepper** to taste

Instructions

1. **Preheat Oven**: Preheat to 375°F (190°C).
2. **Sauté Mushrooms**: In a pan, sauté chanterelles until tender. Season with salt and pepper.
3. **Prepare Filling**: In a bowl, whisk together cream, eggs, and cheese. Stir in sautéed mushrooms.
4. **Assemble Tart**: Pour filling into the pie crust. Bake for 30-35 minutes until set and golden. Cool slightly before serving.

Enjoy these delightful dishes!

Wild Raspberry Smoothie

Ingredients

- **1 cup** wild raspberries (fresh or frozen)
- **1 banana**
- **1 cup** yogurt (or plant-based alternative)
- **1 tbsp** honey (optional)
- **½ cup** milk (or plant-based milk)

Instructions

1. **Blend Ingredients**: In a blender, combine wild raspberries, banana, yogurt, honey, and milk.
2. **Blend Until Smooth**: Blend until smooth and creamy. Adjust sweetness if needed.
3. **Serve**: Pour into glasses and enjoy immediately.

Oak Leaf Lettuce Wraps

Ingredients

- **8-10 oak leaf lettuce leaves,** washed and dried
- **1 cup** cooked quinoa or rice
- **1 cup** mixed vegetables (like bell peppers, carrots, and cucumbers), diced
- **¼ cup** hummus or your favorite spread

Instructions

1. **Prepare Filling**: In a bowl, mix cooked quinoa or rice with diced vegetables.
2. **Assemble Wraps**: Spread hummus on each lettuce leaf, then add a scoop of the quinoa mixture.
3. **Wrap and Serve**: Roll the lettuce leaves around the filling and serve as a fresh snack or light meal.

Wild Fennel Risotto

Ingredients

- **1 cup** Arborio rice
- **1 small onion,** diced
- **3 cups** vegetable broth
- **1 cup** wild fennel fronds, chopped
- **½ cup** Parmesan cheese, grated
- **2 tbsp** olive oil
- **Salt and pepper** to taste

Instructions

1. **Sauté Onion**: In a pot, heat olive oil and sauté onion until translucent.
2. **Add Rice**: Stir in Arborio rice and cook for 1-2 minutes until slightly toasted.
3. **Cook Risotto**: Gradually add vegetable broth, one ladle at a time, stirring frequently until absorbed. Continue until the rice is creamy and al dente (about 20 minutes).
4. **Finish**: Stir in wild fennel fronds and Parmesan cheese. Season with salt and pepper before serving.

Dandelion Wine

Ingredients

- **2 cups** dandelion flowers, cleaned (no green parts)
- **1 gallon** water
- **3 cups** sugar
- **1 lemon,** sliced
- **1 orange,** sliced
- **1 packet** wine yeast (optional)

Instructions

1. **Prepare Flowers**: In a large pot, bring water to a boil. Add dandelion flowers, lemon, and orange. Remove from heat and let steep for 24 hours.
2. **Strain and Sweeten**: Strain the mixture, pressing to extract as much liquid as possible. Stir in sugar until dissolved. If using, add wine yeast.
3. **Ferment**: Transfer to a fermentation container and let sit for 1-2 weeks, covered with a cloth. Bottle and age for a few months before enjoying.

Pickled Wild Onions

Ingredients

- **2 cups** wild onions, cleaned and chopped
- **1 cup** vinegar (white or apple cider)
- **1 cup** water
- **½ cup** sugar
- **1 tbsp** salt

Instructions

1. **Prepare Brine**: In a pot, combine vinegar, water, sugar, and salt. Bring to a boil until sugar dissolves.
2. **Pack Onions**: Place wild onions in a clean jar and pour hot brine over them, ensuring they are fully submerged.
3. **Cool and Refrigerate**: Seal the jar and let cool before refrigerating. Allow to pickle for at least 24 hours before use.

Wildflower Honey Cake

Ingredients

- **1 cup** wildflower honey
- **½ cup** butter, softened
- **2 eggs**
- **1 ½ cups** all-purpose flour
- **1 tsp** baking powder
- **¼ cup** milk
- **1 tsp** vanilla extract

Instructions

1. **Preheat Oven**: Preheat to 350°F (175°C). Grease a cake pan.
2. **Mix Wet Ingredients**: In a bowl, cream together honey and butter. Beat in eggs, then add milk and vanilla.
3. **Combine Dry Ingredients**: In another bowl, mix flour and baking powder. Gradually add to the wet mixture until smooth.
4. **Bake**: Pour batter into the prepared pan and bake for 25-30 minutes, or until a toothpick comes out clean. Cool before serving.

Pine Cone Jelly

Ingredients

- **2 cups** young pine cones, cleaned and chopped
- **4 cups** water
- **2 cups** sugar
- **1 packet** pectin (optional)

Instructions

1. **Boil Pine Cones**: In a pot, combine pine cones and water. Bring to a boil and simmer for 30 minutes.
2. **Strain**: Strain the liquid through a fine sieve, pressing to extract as much juice as possible.
3. **Make Jelly**: In a pot, combine the strained liquid with sugar and pectin (if using). Bring to a boil for 5-10 minutes. Pour into sterilized jars and seal.

Wild Celery Root Gratin

Ingredients

- **2 cups** wild celery root, peeled and sliced
- **1 cup** heavy cream
- **½ cup** cheese (like Gruyère), grated
- **1 clove** garlic, minced
- **Salt and pepper** to taste
- **Butter** for greasing

Instructions

1. **Preheat Oven**: Preheat to 375°F (190°C) and grease a baking dish.
2. **Layer Ingredients**: In the baking dish, layer celery root slices, garlic, salt, and pepper. Pour cream over the top and sprinkle with cheese.
3. **Bake**: Cover with foil and bake for 30-35 minutes. Remove foil and bake for an additional 10-15 minutes until golden and bubbly. Let cool slightly before serving.

Enjoy these wild and flavorful recipes!

Sweet Potato and Foraged Greens Casserole

Ingredients

- **2 cups** sweet potatoes, peeled and sliced
- **2 cups** foraged greens (like wild spinach or dandelion greens), chopped
- **1 cup** ricotta cheese
- **½ cup** grated Parmesan cheese
- **1 egg**
- **1 tsp** garlic powder
- **Salt and pepper** to taste
- **Olive oil** for greasing

Instructions

1. **Preheat Oven**: Preheat to 375°F (190°C) and grease a baking dish.
2. **Layer Ingredients**: In the baking dish, layer sweet potato slices and foraged greens. In a bowl, mix ricotta, Parmesan, egg, garlic powder, salt, and pepper. Spread the mixture over the greens.
3. **Bake**: Cover with foil and bake for 30-35 minutes. Remove foil and bake for an additional 15-20 minutes until golden and bubbly. Let cool slightly before serving.

Wild Sage Cornbread

Ingredients

- **1 cup** cornmeal
- **1 cup** all-purpose flour
- **¼ cup** sugar
- **1 tbsp** baking powder
- **½ tsp** salt
- **1 cup** milk
- **2 eggs**
- **¼ cup** butter, melted
- **2 tbsp** fresh wild sage, chopped

Instructions

1. **Preheat Oven**: Preheat to 400°F (200°C) and grease a baking pan.
2. **Mix Dry Ingredients**: In a bowl, combine cornmeal, flour, sugar, baking powder, salt, and chopped sage.
3. **Mix Wet Ingredients**: In another bowl, whisk together milk, eggs, and melted butter.
4. **Combine**: Pour wet ingredients into dry ingredients and stir until just combined. Pour batter into the prepared pan.
5. **Bake**: Bake for 20-25 minutes, or until a toothpick comes out clean. Let cool slightly before slicing.

Enjoy your delightful dishes!